THE CEREMONIES
OF LONGING

Pitt Poetry Series
Ed Ochester, Editor

The Ceremonies
of Longing

Sandra Kohler

UNIVERSITY OF
PITTSBURGH PRESS

 The publication of this book
is supported by a grant from the
Pennsylvania Council on the Arts

Published by the University of Pittsburgh Press,
Pittsburgh, Pa., 15260

ISBN 0-8229-5830-9

This book is the winner of the 2002 AWP Award Series
in Poetry. Associated Writing Programs, a national
organization serving over 150 colleges and universities,
has its headquarters at George Mason University,
Tallwood House, Mail Stop 1E3, Fairfax, Va., 22030.

For *Walter*

With deep gratitude and warm
affection I would like to acknowledge
Ellen Roberts Young, for two decades of
wise, precise, witty, cogent, and
clear-headed commentary on the
language and structure of my work
in progress.

CONTENTS

I. This Life

II. The Other Hour

III. Tuesday

I.

This Life

This Life

The morning is evergreen, white to pale blue, a sheen
between the branches, on buds, in treetops on the horizon.
In my neighbor's yard forsythia, each long yellow finger
a shock of color. Traffic and the small sounds from the kitchen:
a drawer closing, one spoon against another, the chink of a plate.
I imagine what you are doing and despite all our mornings
together I could be wrong. I could be wrong . . . —to begin
a sentence with that phrase is different than to end it so,
the lucidity of morning different from evening's dark insight.
I want to talk about things too old to describe: forsythia,
marriage. Not about the raw blossomings in the world:
my cousin, eighty-nine now, dying; her son's guilt, sadness;
my brother's "bad winter," drinking. The drone of a plane's engine
meets the dull beginning of a siren's whine. Morning sounds
like night. This will change, it has changed and will again.
It's cold fickle spring, a season on which bloom is wasted.
Spring is always cold and our surprise at it forgetfulness,
a fall over and over into the same trap. What we expect
we learned to expect from something other than experience.
It is like thinking about this life while living it. I write this life
as if there were another; if there were, lived, it would be this one.

The Game

March enters, tossing and drenching winter's dry sticks.
The news of a marriage, of the war ending, seem stories
made up to go with the weather. Because it is March, because
it is morning, in the thawed mud, in culverts under strata
of oak leaves laid down by autumn storms, something is
stirring: the hot green blades of crocuses. Unexpected emergence,
like the cellar door opening and a man dragging his bike out
into the dim sunlight, the mild air. Every day the possibility
opens of some new loss. The two squirrels chasing each other
up and down the bare oak play their game as if it were life
and death and game at the same time, as it is when I play,
tossing away a prize that means nothing and everything.
Like a child learning to skate, I fall over and over into
the same delusion and as I fall, see, no, not again. Now
is when I want to live forever: this morning, this moment.

As I Was

I am the garden hardened
off by sunlight as if sun
were frost: clods resisting
dissolution, here a leaf, mute
brown tongue of the season caught
in the blanketing snow, there purple
flowers pushing into air you can
almost see, breathing the snow.
I'm numb this morning, dumb
with thick voices, silences.
One day every omen will be
predication: future conditional
turned present indicative. Does
circling this mystery do anything but
let us keep distance from it?

What pleasure in symmetry,
matching, your skin against
mine, your flesh. The veins in my
wrist show themselves, sinewy
raised pattern on the white arm. Long
and white and shapely as I was, I have come
to this: the thick fingers of a hand curling
around itself, closing, opening, closing.
Anything more is incidental: the scent
of hair at the nape of the neck, the tender
place at the base of the throat: what marks
us the way God might have touched
Eve's belly, indenting its perfect curved
surface with the dimple one finger
makes to see if dough is fully risen.

Alba

I'm telling you, over breakfast, that the creeping phlox
is starting to bloom, you mutter back something about
the NFL draft, while water boils, pipes creak, April opens
its green eyes like a cat in sunlight, when I remember
scraping the new car along the garage door last night.

The sick sound of metal against wood, worse, how
I seized the occasion, magnified it, scoring us both
with corrosive self-pity, blame. And yet, and yet. . . .
Lying in the bed I made, I felt your body against
mine, my body's waking, the life of its longings.

If I knew the color of the hills this morning, silhouetted
before sunrise, I could name the state we have reached
together, laughing in the middle of the night at a dream,
a joke of the heart's murmur, at nothing, our bodies
softening into each other, aging, imperfect, divine.

Night Music

i.
You tell me one
morning after you'd gone
to bed the night before
leaving me reading on
the couch, that when you
were upstairs, lying in bed,
you thought of getting up,
coming downstairs, thought
you would find me lying on
the sofa, shot through the heart,
as if by the villain in that
mystery I was staying up
to finish. It would be
your fault, because you
didn't say goodnight
to me.

ii.
Woken between one
and two by downpour, rain
splashing into all the southern
windows as if tossed at them,
I get up to close them and sponge
the wet sills, watch till it's let up,
coming down softer, straight.
I raise the windows, take a cold
glass of water up to the bedroom,
sit in the dark at the foot of
our bed. I am there when you
turn in your sleep, reach, touch

the empty place where I'd been
lying, and sleep on. Which of us
will do that some future night,
sleep and dream and reach
for the one of us who has left
behind a space where
we are not?

Love Poem

When I kiss you, I smell earth and potato,
your hands coming out of the cellar,
the potato all eyes growing in the dark.
But last night, the night of the new moon,
which is moonless, I forgot to tell you to look
at the stars, though I'd come in with the words
on my lips. All night my eyes kept opening.
Sleep was where I couldn't stay. The clouds
this morning are all cumulus, all aspire, even
the cirrocumulus, the alto. None of the birds
are alto; they're all soprano, cardinals and
goldfinch at the feeder, monarchs of crimson,
yellow. In this perfectly cloudless dawn, there
is only one star: Venus. The horizon blushes,
hectic, flushed, and above is perfectly blue
after a moment's green yellow. How the day
contrives its distances. Kiss me, kiss me for
each of the years, and I will give you
one star for each kiss, each year.

Sweet

i.

That blue, that green. The green leaves of the small
hickory in the blue green light against the panes. I'm cold,
a lesson in epistemology: shivering, the world I perceive
is a world in which shivering is real. One bird is saying
"sweetie" or perhaps "sweeten" as Lear does, invoking
change in his consciousness. Yesterday a troop of boys,
coming from school, glorious long weekend opening
around them, ran pellmell down the block, stopped,
clustered like bees at a hedge: drinking honeysuckle.
The world sweetened. Now I lie in bed and wrap my feet
in a cotton quilt, remember that in my dream someone
complains of a honey burn. A honey burn: flesh wound, sweet
torment, the sting of having what you cannot keep. I want
to lay my hands on someone's shoulders and hold on.

ii.

I am sitting here like a Buddha; my breasts won't whisper,
the lips of my sex are sealed. What I know and what I live
refuse to marry or separate: a troubled affair neither
can end. Somewhere someone is getting off a train, walking
through thick woods into rose fields where the gorge opens
and waters fall into a pool cut by centuries. I am one of
the boys standing on rocks twenty feet above it, waiting to
plunge. I wake breathing honeysuckle. The garden's a body
like my own, flushed and enveloped by waves of scent.
The azure sky is full of itself, yearning, adolescent.
Something of great delicacy exists in the trough of waves.
I cling to desire, its melancholy, its blue sufficiency.

Sunlight

The sky opens along the horizon,
an oyster's radiant shell. At my son's lesson,
Here comes the sun, four words over and over,
teasing, an invitation. My window's double
glazing reflects an extra sun, brilliant central core
without corona, dimmed enough to look at. I am
a bead, a seed of self in a mattress, the weighted-
down stone and concrete mass of existence.
All the innocence of May cannot change
this story. Before the leaf, the leaf itself is flower.
My son walks naked through my house,
all stalk, all stem, but at his groin, flowering.
Wind in the trees tosses a scatter of sparrows.
The mulberry's branches are shaken by desire.
There is a hill behind the hill, across the river,
its gray ghost. I hear myself repeating each phrase,
each sentence as if it needed its echo, a shadow
for the world in which this world is comprehended.

Staring

Sun flooding the porch makes it hard to gaze
over the yard, fields, to hills, the sky's distractions.
I turn my chair, stare instead into the cherries,
dogwood, flowers gone now, another field of green.
On the lawn there are two sparrows, then none. Telephone
wires stiffen, shake, glint in the light, alive with bird.
In the interstices between one layer of cloud and another,
pure light: an arc the sun has claimed, whiter than milk.
The cardinal in the mulberry is teaching the pale fruit
how to crimson. How little I know of what's coming
toward me. This morning I tried to kill a spider
and was glad when it escaped my foot, scurried,
lived. This is the moment too. Out of nowhere,
joy. Illuminating like the splendid Turneresque sun,
a square blotch of pure gold on the gray horizon.
I am ordering the world the way my son still builds
with his Legos, placing the cardinal in the mulberry,
Bucky Miller in his garden seeing what the rain's done
to his young pepper plants, making the sun's early fire—
its skein of rose light lacing the clouds—a dead painter's
invention, staring this corner of chaos into perspective.

Swimmers

Silence for days. The day for which we are silent is the midsummer
         one
that dawns breathless, already bleached of color by the thick haze
shielding the sun. Upstairs my husband sleeps, my son, my son's
         friend.
All of us stayed up into the hot night, the hot morning; now they
         sleep
like swimmers who have flung themselves down on shore and slept
where they lay. I woke and fought the desire to sleep. The house is
         full
of the dulling sound of fans, a slow acceleration of blades, ebbing
         back
to silence. Already in the streets there is noise, car doors, the
         thrown
paper hitting the pavement. The car starts, papers land, the street is
empty again except of the woman who came out to see if the noise
changed morning. If I stay as close as I can to what happens it will
change. I will understand the underside of what I do each moment,
I will be less afraid of dying. Unsuspected emotion transforms us—
a turning shoulder, a shudder, a ripple in water. The world on the
         banks
is dense, fertile, tributary: everywhere morning's river thickens. I
         am
what moves on the bank. I pick up parts of myself dropped on the
         shore.
I can come to the water slowly, a bride, or running, a child, but I
         can't
stay away. The river moves through like a woman who wants to be
anywhere but in the future, the only place she is sure she is going.

Scene from the New House

This morning a cardinal flashes across the yard. Do you, reading
these words, think I'm not saying what kind of morning
it is? It is gray, serene. I'm tired from last night's lovemaking,
our first since moving. After, we each putter, unpacking
books, papers, a desk's disorder. Our son is "gaming"—role-playing
with a group; when at eleven we pick him up, he's reeking
of cigarette smoke, which he violently hates, saying
it's fine, it didn't bother him. In the kitchen till midnight, talking,
trying not to grill him, but to ask enough. He's walking
into a world we can't enter. I go to bed and wake hearing
thunder and heavy straight rain, a rain reminding
me of ropes. I worry about health insurance and dying. Aching,
grainy-eyed, my back sore, at dawn I sit in the black chair, staring
at the long rectangle of glass that used to be a door, having
palpitations, here, in the new life, watching the cardinal's scarlet
landing.

Overnight

Did the overnight train from Barcelona
to Seville arrive safely, or derail, crash, plunge
into a ravine at sunrise, bearing my son? Ours
was a night of storms, lightning plunging streets
into darkness, thunderous curtains of rain.
Morning rolls down like a stone. I pick it up,
carry it up the hill again: water that's dried
in the plant's pot, the seed birds have consumed,
the empty feeder, larder, heart. The cavity in
the chest must be filled or the body caves in on
itself, husk, sad dry leaving. Leaving. We do it
again and again, like trees, like trains. Clocks
traced in our cells, clocks on walls of the station
for a journey that shapes our ends, tell us it is
time. Three birds on a wire face me, fates. What
have I spun, what have I woven, what have I sewn?
A shroud for my unfinished life, rituals to ward off
death's ambushing disasters. The rain which woke
with me has stopped, I could walk through it
and stay dry. I don't know what task to pick up,
what stone to roll uphill. On another continent
my child is smiling my oldest brother's grin,
suffering my hidden fears, living the life
of a body whose desires I can't imagine.

Floaters

The clouds are floaters and the birds
and the small motes on the screen of my vision

and seeds that drift away from their clusters
to catch and cling where wind takes them.

I am trying to escape my body, my life,
dreaming a time-lapse montage, unfolding

implantation, growth, birth, the flowering
of possibility's shoot. Something will open

for me like the clearing across the river, Shade
Mountain, with its one patch of meadow,

a field to be labored in. I do not say will open
in me. If I assent to this, will I accept any

future? The sky is filling, a faint flush under
the clouds' surface. The river beneath the sky casts

light, reveals its currents. The only drift I know is
in my blood; my seed is spent, its future the white

body of my son. The days hover and brood,
the days unroll a river, the days astonish

like the moon behind the black body of a cloud
formed like a colossus and claiming the sky.

Valentine

This morning I'm thinking about the girl
who's surprised that Shakespeare imagined
cosmic laughter, I'm worrying that my life
is about to provide occasion for the cosmos's
comic faculty. Listing symptoms, I give them,
a Valentine, to my doctor, that holder of hearts.
Why these moments of the failure of courage,
dull resonance beneath a hollow and empty breast,
the voice of a stone in earth? What do I know
about my heart? We are pulses: systole,
diastole, surges like sap, then lapses: an ebbing
wash, power withdrawn. Yesterday was the day
my desires first abated and tomorrow they will
spring up again, living, incongruous. This diagnosis
cannot be confirmed. There is danger here.
Foam laces along the soaked and glistening
sand; transparent bubbles receding, breaking,
one by one, disappear into its grains.

Morning, the Fifth of July

Reaching the window in time to see sunrise:
the glowing disk over the gray hill, bisected by
cloud, burning gold, whole for moments, now
disappearing, eaten by gray. After a day of being sad,
unearned grace. A small burst of birds goes over,
black fireworks on blue, like last night's showers—
rose, green, white on black,—the full moon orange
and low, and over the field among the trees fireflies'
echoing flash, glitter. Everything's sudden, surprise:
the white cat walking up the garden path as if he
belongs, a blackbird's ragged flight, sun piercing
the gray scrim of cloud like a girl rising from the river.
Pray for what you can't want; practice not wanting
what you have. Give the day its task, single, simple:
water the plants, sweep the porch, clean the glass
that separates you from the sun, the moon, the fireflies.
Don't forget what you never learned: how to be here.

Distance

What distant music wakes me, shimmers into sound?
The pines outside throw themselves before the wind,
the mesh of sunlight on the wall glitters, fractured,
mosaic shade and brilliance. I think, "what if I knew?"
then, "I know nothing." This morning I taste a woman's
kindness, a man's impatience. The kindness feels like a blow,
the impatience a cold wall. I erected the wall, I struck
the blow. I rest on these ungrounded assumptions
the way I lie on my bed mornings, drinking my coffee,
spilling these words. What I practice is a craft based
on questions that have not been asked. Where does it
come from—matrix, small hard nub that forms slowly,
densely, a growth under the skin? A web of thread
patterns the cotton shade, thick here, thinner there,
a lattice the sun blooms through. Memory is a lattice;
time a shaft of sunlight. The sudden concerto
of birdsong in sunfilled pines says food, says seed,
says joy, says discovery. If I kept going now where
would I come out? On that stony coast where black rocks
are shattered by white water? Or at the ravine, the river
that leads only down, the mouth of the rocks opening,
cave's cry that cannot be uttered, a music beyond need?
A need beyond music shows me the third way, built
of the dazzling white clay of mountains in the distance
that fade into sky: white clay, white sky, white sun.

Sleep Calls Me . . .

Sleep calls me, the voice of a forgotten lover.
Whose bones would he have me lay out but
my own? The birds' exquisite warblings are
a design embroidered on morning's gray ground.
To run or walk or write? If I run, will I fall
through a rift in morning, into the river,
the creek, the alley, the mud? The cardinal
has come back to nest in the old cherry tree
where the woodpecker lives. Black crest on
crimson, crimson on black and white. If I walk,
I will see the river and make it mine, the geese,
the mallards, the great blue heron rising over it,
all wings. Writing, I find what I am, line by line,
the way we construe the names of the future
out of a dead language. Tell me it's Friday,
it's holiday, peace. Tell me it's the grayest day
of the year. Who am I addressing in these
elegies but necessity, the silent god? Where
there is a green shoot, a seed is being split,
rent, forced open, forced into light.

The Moment

Blue gray, damp, vague—September
morning is banal with small desires: sleep,
hunger, self-doubt's rehearsals. Where
to plant the butterfly bush, the new
dogwood, the aster you want to bloom
this fall? Should you have written that letter
or held your tongue, allowed the friendship
to lapse? In August wildflowers along all
the roads are yellow, gold: pale mullein,
goldenrod, black eyed Susan's blaze:
summer's end catches fire. You begin
to see there's something you won't have;
you want it still. You watch the neighbors
do what they do every morning; you don't
know why they do it, but the recurrence,
like a dream's landscape, reassures: a known
structure against which mysteries are enacted,
the self you are becoming written into being.
How do you know if any moment of grief
is pure? Mourning is shot through with self.
You long for time, not patience. In five years,
the dogwood will bloom profusely.

The Cure

Waking before dawn in a motel in a strange city
from a dream in which I am exploring its dark
streets, I see the wet umbrella in the bathtub,
remember arriving soaked and clammy from
a drought-ending day's worth of cold rain,
wrapping myself in the bedclothes, drinking wine.
What comes back then are those nights years ago,
in the months after I'd left my husband, when
each day I allowed myself one scotch at bedtime,
as if by a prescription written to let me lie down
alone and sleep, my measure of loneliness answered
by that measure of oblivion, taken neat. A pure ritual:
one drink only, never more, taken without fail.
I was my own physician, patient and understanding:
I knew I'd been broken and needed to heal. Each
night's sleep was anodyne I steeped in—or was it
a placebo keeping my disease at bay? Older, sadder,
happier, I could not treat myself with such decisive
will, the rigid discipline of youth, unbending,
dogmatic. I binge, starve, sleep or wake as terror
and the craving for oblivion wax and wane like tides,
extreme as summer's months of drought, last night's
flooding antidote. Loss, anguish, fear of dying
alone, of living alone: all recur; no cure, no cure.

Displacement

The woman in green and the woman with
the dog pass in the alley, striding in opposite
directions. The paths we walk are mirrored by
the paths of our conception of walking, a map
written on and through the mind's cells. Myriad,
labyrinthine, the twisted streets of old towns
dense and chaotic with unchecked growth.

Smoke pours out of a barrel in the yard, drifts
to the creek. Visiting your previous life, you find
the neighbors aren't at home, or they are, but
someone is visiting, wearing your mask; you can't
find another face to present yourself with. You
are in their landscape and out of it like birdsong
or ashes; you've forgotten how to root, grow.

The trees are shuddering, flickering like
shadows, a rare disturbance under the leaves.
I can't tell you what your life was about, or
why it has vanished like the air beneath you
in dreams, sudden vacancy. All I know
insists on being cold summer, green and
disdainful as the bride of circumstance.

II.

The Other Hour

One Music

Last night at the dinner party, talk, starting small,
becoming one music. I replay the sounds, the range:
facile lies, cacophony of minor truths. Staring into
the mirror, I see the lamp over my shoulder,
the reflected wall gray, not amber, the lit hourglass
above and below the lampshade. I am shivering
with desire, and with fear, desire's counterpoint.

Cool fog morning turns to white sun, afternoon
to yellow light, pervading my body, changing
my eyes. In the long corridor between will
and act, intention thins to a liquid transparent
as night's fine rain. This discovery requires
no action, only passion: the power to undergo,
a wet road spread like a veil beneath cars.

The lives of others sound a discourse I can't
resolve, can't resist. I want to shut down memory,
lie above its body like mist over the river, blurring
what's there. I hear only what I've heard so often
I know what's coming, forget not to listen. Isolate,
distant, I conceal my life, its incomprehending
music spinning out flawed, erratic, glistening.

Mother of Thousands

Mother of Thousands: a vine, usually a house plant,
which propagates by putting forth runners with "babies,"
small circular leaves at the end of each . . .

I walk through the Mercer Museum with my son:
cornucopia of the world's work, the tools of all trades
ranged, labor, birth, marriage, harvest threshing,
the gallows and the hearse. We breathe fumes
familiar as milk, bearing taints, tastes, essential oils
from generation to generation, our hoarded past
to the mouth of each morning. I walk outside,
wanting to scrub my face, the crevices of my brain.
"I finally killed my mother of thousands," a woman
in the courtyard is saying. As if women cannot bear
the casual fertility of their kind: everywhere we look
we face something the mother of thousands spawned:
fabric, clay, paper, metal forged, molded, wrought
by her hands, wrists, shoulders, arms. A wish issuing
from her fingers puts out runners: children, houses,
cities; an endless chain, burgeoning's architecture.

Renovo

In the streets of Renovo the past
is soot, a fine pervasive grit that blacks
every surface, the coal that fuelled
its engines ground to meaningless
remnant, a smear of used energies.
What dirty old rags are burning?
The architecture of desire is redrawn
at every stage of knowledge. What we
hope for ourselves, for our children,
for the children we imagine our children
conceiving changes like the blueprints
of cities over a century: expansion,
contraction, the real impinging. Today's
weather is white and hot, unforgiving
as stones underfoot. In Renovo nothing
is forgiven. Sol Marks' son, young Sol,
an old man, tends his father's store,
surrounded by boxwood, mountains,
dirty brick, the dust of August settling
already in June. When his father lived,
his uncles, it was a railroad town, its back
turned to the river, its face to the acres
of yards where engines were repaired,
the calligraphy of lines that carried men
to capitals, cities, another life, daily.
Don't let my children live in Renovo:
town that has lost its lungs, heart, engine
and gazes, hollow, at the brick
monuments of its losses.

Birds and Others

After a hot afternoon, the night is thick
with the green burning of brush, weeds;
silent flashes of heat lightning; suspended hush
of smoke. People come out of their houses, alone
or in pairs, walk through the haze, bodies moving
in the light clothing of summer, the night
clothing them, heat, the crickets' burr
and buzz. The town's a hive, a nest.

Do my neighbors imagine themselves
observed, as I do, inventing the audience
before which I am witness, not yet accused
of any crime, still required to exculpate myself?
Two birds cross my field of vision, one heads
north, one south; their flights cancel each other,
as if caught in stasis, in one moment of stillness
in the sky that is liquid and opalescent.

Something in me won't get free, roam,
is grounded in this place the way for days
now I've been digging one spot in the garden,
rooted. My arms ache as if they'd strained
to embrace something too difficult to hold:
the large regret of rivers, dumb righteousness
moving the plates, the planet. There's more
to the story: light flashing and slowing,

brilliance that glides to a stop and just is,
there on the tarmac, landed the way ducks do,
bracing their webbed feet, a jutting wedge
skimming along the water. Geese fly overhead,
mocking the lines we draw to delineate place.
They have given up going south or north, forgotten
migration's paths; they cleave to this island
that will feed them summer or winter.

Real Estate

The dream has everything: murder, sex, corruption,
real estate. The impossibly ugly summer cottage
we are being shown is the one where days before
the body was discovered. Having read the *Voice*'s
scoop I know not only this but also that the woman
whose taste and housekeeping I regard so disparagingly
has had two husbands, several lovers; that her current
spouse, who as I tour his digs croons in the shower,
screws around; that they were shocked at coming
home to find their dear friend throttled; they
can't imagine what he's done to end this way.

The dirt accumulates like falling water, pooling
in an undrained swamp. The politicians this corpse knew
are legion; his presence here the night he died part
of a scam. Our realtor hardens for the sell: the views,
the size, the sickly trees that could be sentries in a siege,
the quaint appointments in the nursery. We reach
the room where the body was found, scrubbed now,
reeking of Lysol as if some nesting primipara
spent her last gravid days eradicating every hostile
organism from the air her child will breathe.

Descending a sandy hillside, steep as a ravine,
I realize that the life the bland and stylish realtor's
selling me is murder: she's the serial killer, strangler
of the sleazy corpse. This kid couldn't choke a budgie,
my mind says, as if awake, but here she's frightening,
and I am frightened, as the victims she ensnared were not
and could not be, until the struggle, when it is too late.
I flee, the hill erodes beneath my feet; suddenly I am

flying, touching a foothold and soaring up, alighting
further down the slope. Even dreaming I claim
the violence of this world is immaterial as its lease.

Envy

The hard faced woman knocking at my door
to pick up her son—he's playing music with mine—
looks me over as if she were the appraiser
appointed to audit my life. She bristles
like a bundle of sticks tied with rough cord,
each aimed in a different direction, each
menacing one of my eyes. When I offer her
a drink, she takes water, sips as if I've given her
a greasy glass, liquid warm with my spittle.
I want to tell her look, you're right, I have
everything it's not fair—but it's not the chestnut
woodwork or the tiffany lamp or the old quilt
on the wall, it's what spills over the lip of a
brimming pitcher, words, work, the grace
of the man I love, the man child I love.
I have been given, I take with every breath.
But listen, the morning waits, tense and
unapproachable, when all I have will be
taken. The knock at the door, the staring face:
she will be like you, a blonde going to fat,
coarsened by years of deprivation, the school
of envy. She'll come with her list, inventory
of blessings; harvester, gleaner, nothing will
escape her comb, her glance, her eye of ice.

Diaspora

Dreaming, my brother
and I at a ceremony we'd never
go to, reciting a tongue we've put on
with black garments, skullcaps.
The rabbi and his wife perform
a charade, exhausted, wan.
We leave before the end;
driving, then a hotel where
the waitress insists we need a drink
and disappears.

What I remember:
the day he drove me to college,
leaving the home that vanished
when I left; trips from college,
heading north to ski. He'd steer
one-handed, conduct the convertible's
Beethoven thunder. Once
in New Hampshire on a winding road,
we couldn't go on: we stopped in the snow,
the dark; precisely, calm, he turned
the car, skidding at every inch
toward the drop.

I don't remember where
we got to, where we slept that night,
just turning, slipping toward the edge
in the white blizzard fall.
The country of my dream is flat,
the road not dangerous;

there is half-light, a remnant,
no more than we need. We are
smaller, spent. We find
the place for sleep.

The Pond

Why does a man decide to build a pond
on the land of a house he's planning
to sell, a Vermont schoolhouse? Too ashamed
of this decision to tell his wife of forty years,
he calls the contractor, hires him,
commits himself, his shame equaled
by his insistent will: this pond must be.

He should dig the pond himself: fire
the contractor, send away the bulldozer,
the backhoe, begin to spade the thin hard
dirt of Vermont farmland covering the ribs
of stone underneath the way skin covers
an old stringy horse. The pond will come
from the belly of the farm, the loose bowl
of its pelvis. Earth under the hard dry soil
will turn muddy, dense, not friable, still
hostile to the spade, studded with rocks.
It will take days to get down to water.

This man needs to take days. He needs
to sweat in the hot thin October sunlight,
the days that start in cold fog, burning off
slowly, then getting hotter and hotter;
his body, cold in the morning, moving slowly,
by noon hitting a rhythm he puts aside,
sitting down, his back against a tree, to eat
bread, to drink. Then in the short afternoon,
four hot hours, sweating and bending,
his body finding something he thought

it had lost. He must sweat it out
of himself, create the pond, digging it
out of the earth, out of his body.

The End of the Gulf War

The aunts can't believe the war is over. My husband's
aunts, eighty-eight and seventy-seven, each living in her
widowed house within miles of the farm they were born on:
survivors of a harsh childhood among siblings who didn't all
live to adulthood; marriages that spanned a depression, wars;
each the loss, within months, ten years ago, of her husband.
Now the aunts let us take them out to dinner. Aunt Frances
slips into our Honda's backseat like a girl, Aunt Murline needs
help getting her bad leg over what she calls a running board—
like a horse too old to lift its leg to be shoed, she says. We drive
to the cheap restaurant with its more or less honest Dutch food
where they eat a little, always have dessert, talk a little, and steal
the check. Aunt Murline wonders if she'll die waiting for the
     Moravian
Home to find room for her; she can't bear another summer in
her Main Street house, already sold to the bank next door.
They'll tear it down for a parking lot a month after she's out.
We talk about her plans to "make sale" up at the auction house;
we talk about the war. The aunts can't believe the war is over,
it's always been unreal to them, violating their sense of what
the world is like: we act and act, untouched by consequence,
proud of doing well what we should not do at all.

The Aunts

i.
Three old women, sisters but each of them
different. Aunt Geraldine, her stories wild,
detached, living somewhere inside the huge
body, her thin line of a mouth, darting eyes.
Aunt Murline still pretty, under it strong,
a little coarse, with her soft dirty laugh. When
we walk into her room in the nursing home
she has company, a small quick old man
with a walker. They're speaking the language
of her childhood, flirting, keeping company.
Aunt Frances, the baby, at seventy-seven,
childless widow, woman who lives and moves
alone; dancer, her body thickening but
slim legs muscled, hands nimble, woman
you imagine not wanting to be touched.

ii.
The three aunts are the wise women:
the sharp aunt of calculated acceptance,
the soft aunt who placates the hard ladies,
the busy aunt who outruns them.

iii.
The three aunts' song to the young
is siren: we will tell you everything we know
you are thinking, all the small upheavals
of the body we have lived, the bold
rebellions, desires hidden by the skin.
We will populate the small towns

of your origins with all we knew
of ourselves: the pretty girls hot under
their skirts, the thrusting boys.

iv.
The three aunts serve that other three:
the one-eyed aunt of losses, the blind
aunt of the body's failure, the unsleeping
aunt of solitude. Each cold-handed dame
has a pack of hounds, a whip, a scourge.
Each has an iron grip, mechanical hand
that can't be shaken off. Listen, they say,
and worship: we are necessity's hags,
expounding the etiology of aunts.

Divination

Hanging above the horizon before sunrise, the morning
star, the crescent moon: divine twins, Venus and Diana.
Sisters. Brother sun's beneath. Aunt Cloud stretches her
lean strong body along the eastern rim. Stars, planets,

the crystalline dark rising like a shade. I'm cold and clear
as the rooftop's pool of ice. We read the skies askew, wanting
one prediction confirmed: we matter. Why do our daughters
turn harridan, our sons sullen as old babies? Flocks of birds

thicken southwards, the voices of light. It's hard to write
to someone who won't read. It's hard to talk to someone
who won't grieve. All night I slept and woke and slept and
woke—somewhere this progression ends on the wrong note.

Memory is like this: the black garden, the sky that is
no longer black, the knowledge that change can't be seen
when it's happening. How is memory like this? I can't
remember. When I do it will be different, not like this.

Dreaming Jane Eyre

If the brown spider I find in my bed this morning
were black, would it be sinister, widow? *Vedova*—
soft word with a hard sound at its core. Cruelty
has nothing to do with being hard. Alone in this house
I possess it and forget that the nature of possession
is blind, deceitful. I manipulate my body, the light,
the sounds, my dream. What I do here is fill a page;
in the night, a space in the logos of dreamers.
What is important happens just beyond me: I have
arrived without luggage, clothes; I wear another
woman's discarded garments and want to keep them.
Shopping underground I find racks and rows of shoes,
bags, sunsuits I remember from an earlier season.
Then there are the thin Italian shirts. These dreams
conceal and reveal; they fall open through hidden
plackets, disclose the unexpected given: wild card
dealt by some power, brown spider in my bed. I am
teaching *Jane Eyre* and cannot find in anyone's copy
the scene in which Jane tells Rochester he may rape her
but still will not possess her. I'm determined to read
this aloud, but Jane is driving over a bridge that
narrows to an end, surrounded by waters. All
the words for what I find are in another language,
saying themselves on my tongue the way I try out
Jane's dream. It is the beach at Rimini, a story
breaking instead of dawn over the yellow sand.

Second Language

Struggling to speak the language of my accusers,
painstakingly, in awkward French, I concede my guilt,
my regret, the reasonableness of my attacker: *vous avez*
raison, je regrette beaucoup. . . . I am in Paris, and I have
acquired two cats I must be rid of. Curiosity sits at
my shoulder, curls round my arm. There's no time.
I need to plan, to pack. *Partire, lasciare, uscire*—I remember
Italian verbs for leaving. The day is a road I can't imagine
and want to foretell. Curiosity nuzzles my ankles.
It takes all my wit and all my energy to catch the two—
they elude my grasp, hide in the nooks and crannies
of this big old house. I need to learn a language which
provides words for what I can't find: a new relation
to the world. When I ask the vet if he can find homes
for them, he warns he may have to destroy them, then
summons an old priest who scolds me for having
acquired them knowing I would leave one day. In French
it's *partir.* This is the reprimand I am working so hard
to acknowledge, in a schoolgirl's rusty French. Like
original sin, it can't be denied, must be admitted
in that second language learned in childhood, forming
on the lips with difficulty out of some source beyond
the conscious, never quite mastered, nor quite forgotten.

After Arcadia

On the cusp of the nineteenth century, romantic
meets rationalist. People fancy the wrong people:
Mozartean *ronde*, that sad comedy. Love is the joke
sex plays on us, sex is the serpent in the garden,

and death is the pattern in the garden's leaves.
Iterated algorithms. The first things are morning,
light, mourning. The last things are evening, light,
mourning. Let me discover what is between them:

the light between lights, the bland opening of
afternoon. A door opens that was not there, was not
a door. Mrs. Ramsay could not teach the family to
leave windows open, doors shut. Which windows,

what doors? One lets in sunrise, the other, sunset.
What is caught in my throat, I tell myself, is not
my heart, murmuring. The birds begin. How
delicate the flutter—which bird? Heart.

Museum Piece

A Magritte sky: impossibly fleecy
backlit clouds drift into bluest depths.
At dawn, Chirico: charcoal ominous
cirrus on greeny-pink sea, Venus hinting
her existence. Wordless, I wake to
underworld: anemones, sea blossoms.
My head's a furious place. All occasions
inform: light is occasion, this, this.
The economy of change pares away
necessity, desire: what we know is never
adequate to what we are, what we are
faithful to what we know. As if we'd lost
our origins, our stories, remembered only
moments. A park. A bus. I'm with a man,
I catch the bus and he doesn't. All day
we've walked the park, it's August's end,
green, cold, bleaker than November.
One of us is leaving. The bus stops in front
of the museum where, for years after, what
I look at in a painting is the sky. Everything
changes as we know it. Magritte's sky doesn't
move as this one is moving: scrolls like light's
signature written on cloud, disappearing.
Birds speak, a walker I see every morning
passes. The seasons' grave lies under my skin,
in cells my throat has swallowed a hundred
times. My thighs are dryads, saplings waking
in the dead of winter, knowing only
that something in them must rise.

Recapitulation

Waves of sleep and the desire for sleep flower like
the sky's skein, gray and blue, white cirrus etched.
In my dream, you forgot it was Monday, not Sunday,
that parking is illegal, the hotel will charge extra,
the city is alien, you don't have a novel to read.
You are alone and frightened of something I don't
understand. After years apart, our bodies still cannot
do what they couldn't each time we met: refrain
from touching. I can't remember when I've been
so heavy with outworn longing. What has become
of you, you who wondered what would become of me
and lost your own story, or found it diminished as
the gods? Mine goes on, rises in me like water, reaches
down from me like roots. Wind tosses the trees,
branches fling themselves about as if they were trying
to escape. The mulberry is a white cloud in the dark.
A stream of flight breaks gray's monotony, birds
turned yellow and blue bruises on the skin of the sky.
You kissed my shoulder, my neck. Above my heart,
there's a clot of pain I feel darkly, as if I were underwater,
buoyed by a power beyond my will to penetrate:
the body's hard insistence on being body.

Celebration

There are parts of the past that seem complete, like that
black dress you always have one of: through its banal magic,
disguise, you become what everyone believes you. Others
are like the dream close to waking, when, dreaming, you
wake hearing shouts, choruses of uproar, anger, laughter.

I am walking down a hallway, bleak, saddened. I know each
day is gone forever. I see my friend's husband, for a moment
think I'll let him comfort me. When he turns into another room,
I don't follow. John arrives, carrying a tuba, Ellen with a lacy
straw hat. Inexpressibly jaunty, they come into the hallway,
leading the band they've formed, playing for some anonymous
birthday, anniversary, festival of a religion with the courage
for joy. I am sent to buy cakes at a store where beggars
lying on black sidewalk gratings refuse the alms I offer.

What happened, with whom, vanishes. The image gone, effects
in the body remain. Thoreau was wrong: new clothes may be
selves we hadn't imagined. How else have I learned this music?

Primary Colors

The music is common, inherent, residing in ordinary
nouns and verbs, plain syntax. The red truck, the yellow
bus, the blue convertible. The tossing breeze in the shrubbery.
The sky this morning: blue and delicately marked as if pawed
by some great animal leaving traces. But at the east, a pearl's
luminous curve, gray opalescence. The red light of the sun
and the white light of the moon feed multitudes. The woman
in the blue skirt, the woman in the red dress, the woman in
a black kimono spotted with roses, outraged unhappy flowers.
I have been given a key, yellow as the sun, a red envelope.
Put the key in the envelope, hand it to the woman in blue
and it opens a door, to the woman in red and it seals her past,
to the woman in rose-strewn black and it turns the lock
of a tomb. Someone is cutting flowers; the snap of the shears
beheads them, a small sharp guillotine. As long as the narrative
lasts, there will be a thread to hold on to, cotton like the weave
of a summer dress you sew in deepest winter. Like the boy
in the dark, we experience delight at our fingertips, but can't
claim it. All our imagining cannot foretell the infinite future
of tears and children; the bitter taste of the real, or the sweet.

The Other Hour

The Chinese restaurant whose ads I heard for years
on the classical station without going there existed,
whole and realized, in my mind, bearing no resemblance
to the one I finally saw when I did go. But the Mandarin
in my mind didn't disappear, banished by the actual;
now there were two. Days unfold in our minds before
we live them, hours we hope for, fear. All day I've known
at midnight I will be afraid, anxious, walking through
the house waiting waiting seeing my son's body, a man's
now, shattered; the small sportscar under the semi,
crushed metal piercing the Piero feet, the Botticelli
thighs. Yet it is midnight, he has arrived early; he stretches
long legs bruised blue and ochre playing soccer, he eats
Chinese leftovers, he describes driving up a mountain into
cloud and what the moon said when he howled at it.
The imagined hour is here and different. The hour
I conjured is also here, it has shaped what the bruises
on his legs could narrate, what the length of him
owns in my house, how his father is pale.

III.

Tuesday

After

Home. After the snow, the wind, the rain.
After the arrival like old lace, the kiss
like that of an old woman, soft, surprised:
home. The birds matter, even the finches
and sparrows. The commonest dun feathers
are myriad brown gray black white, inwardly
glowing spun thread of something alive.
They are the harbingers of some harvest I haven't
yet claimed. Circumstance reigns like a trollish
god, reins me in, rains out the gullies of old habit.
In my garden I have planted hydrangea paniculata
grandiflora, autumn's garland. Will it bloom
next year, great panicles of white that flush and
dry in late summer like the soft rouged cheeks
of an old woman? Nothing prepares us for the real,
the future's long embrace of change. The fields
bring us their flowers, those fine upstanding
specimens, milkweed, Queen Anne's lace, stiff
yarrow. They throw down their seed like weapons,
they surrender to grass. The inn of achieved
happiness waits at a bend in the road. Today
sings in its coffin, tomorrow. The first snow,
the first thaw, were never this surprising. Home.

The Lie

Nothing my body says can be
untrue. More and more I inhabit it
the way I do this room, this house,
making it more my own daily.

I have taken root at this window,
sat here so long morning after morning
my eyes are connected to the line
of the hills, my feet reach down like
willow roots, till they drink the creek.
A dove perched on the telephone wire
sways a little, shows her pale breast,
mourning dove, the colors of
autumnal morning, fawn, pearl.

In rooms of my house I have yet
to discover I dream there are boxes
of good earth, and in them, earthworms
burrowing. I am not happy to have
so much life in my house. Nights
I lie torn between the body's deep
autumnal wish to lapse into itself,
give way, cede itself to itself, its dark
final processes, its caged
passionate protest.

Tell me where I am going and why
and I won't believe you, my cells
insist the story is endless, open as
the horizon, younger than yesterday's
spilling seeds. My cells lie, every
atom, false to the core.

Burden

Bird swaying in a branch of the mulberry, black bundle
I feel in my throat, under my breastbone. The creek
out of its banks, swollen, seeping into the fields, rushing
through weeds, bracken, shrubs, around the trunks
of thick willows, great rooted mouths that drink their
fill and drink and stay. The water's insistence matches
the willows'. I sit at my window and observe those who
do not know I observe them. Even face to face with love,
I watch someone who does not know I am watching.
Love's touch all over my body wakes my body: the breath
that animates dead clay. When the door opens there is
always someone there: little sister feeding on the stories,
an untamed animal learning to stay. Bondage is never
only external and what I take from my ropes knots my
own cells. The fine mechanisms of the body are thrown
off by a random glance, a breath. My flesh knows I am
medium: the green bird summer cannot see, camouflaged
by leaves. I am older than summer, more generous
than fall, I will be crueler than winter.

Augury

The cloud of unknowing hangs over
the river, blue and cold. All of us wear
knives but use them only to cut each other
out of traps. No apologies, no forgiveness.
Don't forget that the pagans among you
are just as profane as the Christians. Send
the flesh and the blood into remission,
obscuring old ceremonies. Honey and
oranges won't do; eat bread and water.
Heaven holds me, holds you. Is not what
we think. Ether, medium, never destiny.
Only what's open can be claimed, entered.
Live what cannot be resolved until it can
be turned away at the facing doors which
let in sunrise, sunset: the beached event
of cloud, the dark gathering. Languor and
hardening, crimes of the heart. The heart
of the crime is its simplicity: what you
should have done and didn't become a gap
in possibility. Desperation is a passing
glance. This clarity is more than morning.
Black hills surface from fog; the green sky
turns red gold: a cold kiss of arrival. All
morning the morning will be visible as noon.
There will be clearing, sharp sun, knife blade
air; there will be no way not to suffer.

Beasts

Great clouds have come to lie down along
the horizon like grazing beasts, burdens. Dawn's
rose flush, pale rise of fog off the river vanish;
the sky darkens, despite the sun's white insistence.
The month, the season nearing an end, frost's
astonishment waits, stunning plunge. The zinnias
on the table are the last I will cut. A long car passes,
slow and silent, as if training us to follow. Every
echo reveals a wall. When what we hear answers
our unspoken wish with the flat antidote of denial,
we know we are grounded in the real. Yellow lamplight
from the white building next door: on brown lawn
the pink dogwood's a blood red shade. Anxiety's
red sky casts an autumnal stain on parched fields,
parquet of straw, clay, chaff: what's left of what
we've lost. When we retrieve our wildness, will we
find it has grown new teeth, new claws, a fine
fur coat? The car returns, tracing its push through
darkness with red eyes. Let me learn to move
like something feral, something clandestine.

Inverno

Breaking damp, bleak, raw-edged:
this is the day, the only given. I dreamed
of a woman I admire, a man I admire less;
marrying them to each other, using their
distinctions against them. Each is less together
than apart. This is a way of talking about
pettiness: someone else's married to my own.
All the long bones in my body are turning
ninety degrees, aligning themselves with
the horizon. The flat *is* dominates landscape.
Sleep comes over me again between the noun
and the verb, preposition and object. I am object,
abject, complex and compound, everything
a sentence can be. Let others talk of dominion;
my kingdom's a breast, a belly. A triangle
of bare skin above my breasts, between them,
grows cold. I cover it with my robe and hope
to outwit sorrow. In Italian hell and winter
are separated by a difference of one letter.
The cadences of my speech betray a similar
coupling. I'm tense, I'm anxious, I'm frightened.
Three states like half sisters, each daughter
of a different father, the same mother: my body.
The last breath of summer just expired under
the leaves, the first bird of winter says its name
and falls silent. This could go on forever.

Litany

Rain this morning is the glazed blue
of the old fruit bowl on my table, a culture's
stab at sky. I wake, a litany of bones betraying
their secret origin in quarries where longing
is a vein running through the white lode.
They are telling me something about time
that I know, something about eternity I can't
take in. There's anger, there's anguish. Put them
in their corners and turn your back. They will
make mouths at each other behind it,
acknowledge each other across it. But how
do you get out of the room and what do
they do when you are gone? The sky's drained
of color, the landscape attenuated, thinned
to the flat fields of existence. La di, la di—
there, over there. That is always where the sound is.
Spell me a while, the bones say, let me go back
to the dumb luck of being inanimate, the white
hope of speechlessness. La di, something answers,
thread of song, voiced consonants grieving
for what morning could be: undetermined,
free of the machinery of recurrence.

Seed

Brilliant blue cold, winter's fastness. One shade
down, one up; a white rectangle, a black. Sunrise:
one faintly yellowed patch in the mauve gray cloud bank
lowering on the horizon; a fat brushstroke of darkness.
I wake so lucid I can't remember what dream I was in.
What's meant for light admits the darkness: dreams,
skin. Our bodies tell us the color of our minds. Order
and harmony exist because a chemical predominates
in a cell. I am just writing down what you say, my *consoeur*.
We are the mothers of sons grown to our height or taller,
how have our breasts produced these bony gangling boys?
It begins in dream, that nursery of all that flourishes,
tiny seed of the real. Read these words and recognize
the voice as your own, the one you forget but hear
under the hiss of radiators, cacophony of awakenings:
bone house chorus. Over and over I invent this instrument
for recording what it is to be living. Pain grips me
and I remember that to be in the body is to be in the grip
of something. Repetition is more than a method: as if
what is underneath is saying its name, trying to reach us
the way after decades perhaps, a season reaches us,
the sugar maples' iridescent yellow and scarlet surges
of sap, the oaks' bronze and crimson arrivals,
the dogwood's blood red flowering.

Counterpoint

This morning it is the frost which is beautiful—
a white skin laid down on the fields, the grass,
the fogged white hills. The sky is masked by furl,
feathering. The pure cold stream of it, snow, fog,
frost. One finch huddles on the porch, puffed out,
nesting in its own feathers. Anything merits light:
the finch, a pair of sparrows. A missing child.
A widow leaving on a cruise. The sad man carrying
his burden to the garage, the young woman with
everything to burn. Birds alight on wires strung
across the yard, perch and swoop, a sudden flurry.
When they are gone the silence thickens, the way
snow drifts over the lawn. Smoke joins the white
arrivals. Above its monochromatic glaze, a dazzle of
sun. Some heaviness, thick sorrow, surfaces, emerges.
How unwilling I am to change. Only morning can be
itself, forgetful, unprepared, without forethought.

Not My Own

Morning, in a bed not my own; I have brought
my coffee up from the kitchen to this cold attic
room, virginal, the bed with its tight heavy blankets,
like Mrs. Dalloway's, the small window, narrow sill,
the watercolor that could be Lily Briscoe's, geometric
shapes, a landscape abstracted. The house is filled
with fragrance, lingering, ineluctable. Outside, the light
on snow, the sheen of ice on the roads; leaves clinging
to trees, persistent oaks. Yesterday, at the funeral,
the pastor can't pronounce Aunt Murline's name.
Cousin George, the undertaker, is outliving the whole
family. A cold clarity binds me the way all night these
blankets bound me to sleep, to dream. Lost uncles and
aunts wander through, call to me; I can't come, I can't
get free. Under the willows and open meadow, a thread,
a trickle moves like light through the bright ribbon
of the creek. The ceremonies of longing play out in
all the households of dawn. The bones of our faces
are prisons, the spinal cord's a solitary chamber. I want
to discover how a rigid woman unbends, a puritan
learns to eat time. On the breast of the snow,
the light breaks with its own weight.

Frostlight

Frostlight, greeny-brown. The hills lost in it, fields
glazed with it. I wake from some deep pool, to sun
surfacing from dense white haze. Smoke rises into
the fog, white on white; the sun's lost, paler, the fog
colder. Ill, I have been a child, with no taste for wine,
coffee, the complex bitter adult pleasures. I sleep
not doubting that I'll wake. At daybreak, the light
is missing that underlies apprehension. The cardinal
stirs in the cherry tree, comes to the feeder, a solitary
flame. The man in red lights the fire that will not blaze
up till he is gone, the gray van passes down the gray
alley, flames go orange, the man in red walks into
wilderness that starts with his first step. Children play
each afternoon in the cherry tree, climbing as if for
life. This is before buds, before the first green thrust
of unripe blossoms. I don't know why the man in red
turned left, why flames in the barrel are racing.
I am needy as soil, clotted and unturned. What if
I created words like crocuses, mostly yellow nouns,
a purple verb, three white adjectives? Light turns
the dust motes on my window to a scattering
of gold. I am left with nothing to say.

It's a Wrap

The sun's lucid attack on day shatters
the sky, shades earth. How? By blinding us
so that light dims, strewn with fields of
darkness. A stick figure, neither man
nor woman, walks down Water Street. Days
pass just this way, swift, hieratic. Somewhere
there must be time opening out, the other
end of the telescope my life forms, numbing,
narrowing. To the south clouds are massive,
a mass of ifs, but the north is clear, a blue
empyreum, absolute as is. The sun is eating
my eyes. A headache heads for the third day,
heeding nothing. I need the heedless spill,
verbing. Someone lived here, someone crept
into the day, someone failed. I don't know what
will tame the lions, I don't care to have them
tamed, but the damned rodents need to come
to order. Whose job is this? Blackbirds peck
at the hard dirt in front of the hovel where
the harpies of bent stew and beaten biscuits
crow an answer: spell a meal, eat your words,
give someone the pleasure of your cacophony.

At the Grave

I'm searching for the place to eat breakfast,
a drugstore with a man behind the counter named
Deacon, bald, enigmatic, stolid, his archaic clipped
speech oracular. Complaint and loneliness, everyone
too busy to spare a cup of cream, a glass of eggy
consolation. The drugstore's under the el, lit from
within like Hopper's, the booths and menus greasy
with use. The floor is covered with what looks like
fishnet but clings like barbed wire, thorny dilemma
I fail to get myself out of. Everything is barbed
and twisted, bent into a shape that could be omen
or ominous. Where I go next is a macadam and
concrete garden, studded with rust-stained white
slabs, a crabapple half-dead, hung with dull red
fruit, home to a flock of dun sparrows that flurry
out as I pass it. On the grave, gifts: a powder puff,
a shell, a piece of bridal cake, balls that hold children's
laughter. What I was is so deeply buried only disaster
excavates: earthquake, tidal wave. For the day's
exegesis, give me my shards, my orts, the dung
beetle's great rolled ball. What misgives me is food,
the rough fodder for a stable of animal fears. Whose
breakfast will I become? Give a girl one break and
she'll fracture the universe to find out how bones
mend. The bones are restless, the rest is bone.

Steps

Everywhere the birds, their voices
in thirsty air noise not song, an edge
of anger, frantic pitch. Eat, eat, they urge
each other, or you will not survive the day.
I who am stepmother waking become
stepchild in dream, humiliated, infantilized.
The injuries of the nursery tell their story
and every one of us is jealous: of the brilliant
children who obscure us, the importunate
ones who muffle our outcry, the radiant
beside whom our skins are dun. Both of
my children, in dream, are favored siblings.
Of what am I deprived? Mother and child,
I have become little again; lacking not stature,
but power: my tiny stepmother buys the child's
ticket she wants me to travel on, though I
protest I couldn't pass for thirty. My adult
journey will not be paid for. Will it prove,
like hers, the long life of the blandly tough,
whom no indignities defeat? Learn her
lesson: forge the egoist's shield, massive
and reflective as Achilles', to wear through
the world. What can be taken from me
will be. Birds at the feeder, on the frozen
wire, chuffing, puffed out against the cold,
are loud and hungry as my dream.

Tea

The sky steeping, dark brew,
the morning star brilliant and alone.
A sense of disorder. The tea turns
green at the horizon, overhead orange,
mauve. Nights what keeps me awake
is a refusal to give in, allow the day
to end. I dream I'm in New Zealand—
purple skies, thunderous ocean.
Standing on line to see "Waiting for
Godot" I find it's become Japan.
I squat at the front of the tiny theatre
with a man I've met in the queue, tell
him I'm happily married but lonely—
my husband's away for a month.
He thinks I'm neglected and I explain
we each do the things we want not to die
without having done. On stage there is
another sky: turbulent sea of cloud,
seams and layers, troughs. Coffee arrives,
time is short. I can't keep awake. I listen,
I speak; it's only a question of language.
I want to be snow bound and cloud free
at once: wind driven, deep rooted.
On the garage roof there's a patch of
snow like the one white blotch on
a black cow's flank, circle, symbol.
The woods are a dark husband,
the meadow the white ghost of
a bride spectral and waiting.

Intimation

Nothing's here but sleep, desire, fog
and snow, a landscape of white becoming
gray, gray becoming white. No geese,
no heralds over the creek or hills to tell us
this hour is sacred, ordained by necessity's
chambered heart. And yet, and yet . . . silence
is absence, absence the intimation of presence.
I am included here. If my dreams spoke,
they would be misunderstood; their language
is so difficult to speak without weeping, and
the tears of things glut the throat. The present
interrogates the past, or is it the past which
forces itself into the present, demanding
its meaning in the now? Someone gives me
a pair of hands, a bone, a seed. Bury what's dead,
bury what will be living. Time's the detective
who sorts, seeks, lists the suspects. Loose,
unhinged, I swing like a door on one screw.
What's sprung me? Don't tether my movements,
my pulse. Loose me, shake me, let me come
loose. The weight of this winter is causing roofs
to collapse, whole buildings to shudder and
fall, slip into rain like an icicle with one shiver.
Why did I think I would go unscathed?
Something in me will buckle, give way, sigh
once under the cold terror of a thick crust
of days and let go. Only the small bones over
my insteps hold me to my soles. The body
is black with longing. Give me my hours,
my long days and nights laid out like paths
in the snow. Give me the kiss on the forehead,

lips meeting a familiar texture of skin, tasting the forgotten salts of affliction. This ceremony will be enough. It will be used, consumed, renewed, made bread and consumed again, like the earth, like everything around us, like us.

Green

The green. The gray. The creek gathers like a young
river, the geese cry out overhead. I am called to sunrise,
to the cold clear sky, to the silver paring of moon,
a comma in the sky's declaration that nothing matters
but the light, growing. Tell the green to talk to the gray.
Push the gray to reveal its inner self to the abandoned grass.
The grass is abandoned because green floats and flies like
fireweed, like racing cars, like the flat road to a waiting sea.
The winter we called extraordinary, one in decades, has
ended. Now the grass is beginning to turn, at this hour
of pure rising light it lies before me steeped in a color
no winter knows, while branches of azalea are strewn,
hearts shattered, the thick upright centers, great bouquets
that should be thrust into early summer like torches.
Nothing matters. The birds begin their chanting, rhythmic,
cold, insistent. I don't wonder about yesterday's snow but
how my heart bears disappearance is more than my sinews
comprehend. I lived in Arcadia, I tasted fruit, I thought
there often of the feel of the creek's silky muddy water,
how under it my skin would look golden, wondered how
cold its shock would be. In the beds I can't see, beneath
my window, perennials are beginning their green journey,
and the maimed azaleas will or will not bloom.

Japanese Landscape

How delicately last night the clouds seduced first
the setting sun, then the rising moon. I should have
cut flowers for you in the rain yesterday. Arrivals
resonate in memory's chambers, cast a light
strange and flaring as the flush on the eastern hill,
orange ghost sun compounded of snow and flame.
In my shallowest dream I am in the kitchen,
wondering what has happened to familiar shapes,
the large bowls on high open shelves. My cupboard's
bare. You are riding your bike down the alley where
the commonest weeds bloom: Queen Anne's lace,
the pokeweed's purple balls of ink, chicory, cornflower.
You will find those veined leaves, those shabby flowers
on the hillside that from this side of the river seems
a gray Mount Fuji, rooted in fog, rising like birdsong,
smoke. Is the buddleia fragrant in this cold mist?
Light washes the horizon, translucent, gleaming
tracery of the risen sun's splendid longing to exist.
The passion of a single bush transforms possibility.
I have watched the butterfly, banded blue and orange
cling to the red violet sprays. I won't die easily.

Tuesday

Tonight we have dreamed in a yoke: one
the image, one the words. In the morning
we exchange news like talismans: you are
naked, teaching more brilliantly than ever;
you can't get back to where your clothes are.
I report what you've said: you hate Tuesdays.
Frost on the fields; over the river, creek, hills,
a sheen mute and glistening. Overhead a scrim
of hieroglyphs drifts slowly northeast, a dark
horse of cloud rides the paler prairie. There's
a walker in the alley; on Water Street, a cyclist,
swift phantom. In the creamy sunlight, you are
walking into the garden, bending to a faded rose.
This morning is Tuesday. I am the one who is
beginning to hate Tuesdays, the nakedness I feel
teaching the Tuesday lesson, which is the pure
mundane, absolute pitch of the daily. How can I
unweave the web of circumstance, the chains
of custom? I want to walk out into the light
beckoning from the fields, out into it and
down to the river, shivering.

After Thanksgiving

Ambivalent light, faded with distance,
filters into the canyons of day's gray city:
opaque arrangements of drift and flow, strata
of shadows on harsh granite. Celebrating
a diminished ritual, we see we are old,
suddenly shrunken figures whose hands,
once masters of ivory and ebony, cannot span
the octaves. The exercise of our days and
powers contracts to rote: a day's travel, then
sleep. Where I travelled in sleep was day's
reflection: the road taken in, become part
of my body, small fears, the humiliation
of being perfectly myself. How will the past
redeem itself now that we are the past?
The body of winter drains to a black and white
sketch: stick trees, stick birds, a coat upon a . . .
This is new, this is the present speaking:
our aging, our new austerity, the dimensions
of what we have learned chastening us.
Ask and it shall be given: one brings bread,
one ripe fruit, one the stew of flesh and
blood: answered anguish, transcendent vision
on the road we take every morning.

Sojourn

The creek is disappearing behind a sudden veil
of leafhaze, yellow green: willow twigs, thickening
buds, new grass spreading a green blush on the face
of the hill. I have set my life aside, a lover whose
desires I cannot grant. I don't have a reed, a plumb
line. The scent of something stale, musty, rises
from dry leaves lying on the breeding earth, from
its crust of hardened topsoil, from those ochre
streaks in the clouds. There are rats in the compost:
are they water rats, barn rats, town rats? We live
in town, on the creek, the river, the waterways
of rat. The rat is one guest, the goldfinch another.
Predator and innocent, frail but brilliant. The sky's
a place where three different cloud landscapes are
stacked against blue hills, paintings standing behind
each other. A stroke of white jet scores through all
three: plumb line. If grass were this virid in winter,
it would be unbearable; we would be torn by a state
of permanent longing. We are ghosts, sojourners.
The inchoate earth is turning. Let go. Let the buds
wither and fall. Live as if you were immortal.

Write

I can never write on the days I have to walk across
the square to buy cigarettes.
—SOMERSET MAUGHAM

Thank you, Ina, for sending me this fine excuse for

the inexhaustible possibilities of laziness,
the unwillingness of body and spirit to write.
The desire for dense bread, the desire for
sleep, the desire for work to be easy—no, hard,
but clear, glassy, transparent, all-revealing.

The work is a series of counterpanes, blankets
you lift, as if looking for the princess's pea. One
day, it's a pair of shoes I've lost: green suede, but
when I find them, they're gold; transformed like
the orts I make poems: pleasure, life and death.

If the shoe fits, I'll get under the covers and
wait to be transformed, hag into queen. I'm wearing
white taffeta, a dress so ugly I put on a teeshirt
to cover it. I will buy black clothes, I will teach
astronomy, I will stop accounting for myself.

Angering my mother, I make rag dolls out of
the family's secret bones. I am hauling myself from
one floor to another of a huge warehouse full of
shorted-out machinery, in a cage I operate by pulley,
bearing my own weight, the weight of the cage.

It's hard to do it all in one trip. There is only
one trip to do it in. We wear the chains we forge
in life, Miss Beryl reminds us. Encaged, jewels
in a setting. Onyx, amethyst, chalcedony.
Can a jewel make its cage golden?

I am writing for time, clarity, the lucidity of parsed
moments. I am writing to leave a small fossil that
says I lived pressed into the medium that killed me.

ACKNOWLEDGMENTS

Grateful acknowledgment is made to the editors and publishers of the following journals, in which these poems first appeared: *Bellevue Literary Review* ("The Cure"); *The Black Warrior Review* ("Primary Colors"); *Calapooya* ("Mother of Thousands"); *The Chaffin Journal* ("The Aunts"); *The Colorado Review* ("Second Language"); *Diner* ("As I Was"); *The Evansville Review* ("Renovo"); *5 AM* ("Celebration," "The End of the Gulf War," and "Night Music"); *Flyway* ("Dreaming Jane Eyre"); *Fugue* ("Diaspora"); *The Gettysburg Review* ("After Arcadia," "Sweet," and "The Game"); *The Journal* ("Intimation"); *The New Republic* ("Counterpoint" and "The Moment"); *Northeast Corridor* ("The Other Hour"); *The Notre Dame Review,* ("After Thanksgiving" and "Distance"); *The Painted Bride Quarterly* ("The Pond"); *The Pedestal Magazine* ("Sojourn"); *Pleiades* ("This Life" and "Sleep Calls Me . . ."); *PMS: poem/ memoir/ story* ("Envy"); *Rhino* ("Tea"); *The Southern Review* ("Litany" and "Swimmers"); *Square Lake* ("Inverno"); *Washington Square* ("Staring").

SANDRA KOHLER is the author of *The Country of Women* (1995) and the recipient of two Individual Artist Fellowships from the Pennsylvania Council on the Arts. Born in New York City, she received her undergraduate degree from Mount Holyoke College and her master's and doctoral degrees from Bryn Mawr College. Widely published in literary journals, Ms. Kohler has taught literature and writing courses at levels ranging from elementary school to university and adult education. She lives in Selinsgrove, Pennsylvania, a small town on the Susquehanna River in central Pennsylvania, with her husband.